The Mysteries of Mithra

By
G. R. S. Mead

Copyright © 2022 Lamp of Trismegistus. All rights reserved. No part of this publication may be reproduced or transmitted in any form or by any means, electronic or mechanical, including photocopying, recording, or by any information storage and retrieval system, without permission in writing from Lamp of Trismegistus. Reviewers may quote brief passages.

ISBN: 978-1-63118-619-6

Esoteric Classics

Other Books in this Series and Related Titles

Aurora of the Philosophers by Paracelsus (978-1-63118-507-6)

Rosicrucian Rules, Secret Signs, Codes and Symbols by various (978-1-63118-488-8)

On the Philadelphian Gold by Philochrysus & Philadelphus (978-1-63118-511-3)

Paracelsus, the Four Elements and Their Spirits by M P Hall (978-1-63118-400-0)

The Stone of the Philosophers by A E Waite (978-1-63118-509-0)

Clairvoyance and Psychic Abilities by A Besant &c (978-1-63118-403-1)

The Rosicrucian Chemical Marriage by Christian Rosenkreuz (978-1-63118-458-1)

The Alchemical Catechism of Paracelsus by Paracelsus (978-1-63118-513-7)

Alchemy in the Nineteenth Century by Helena P. Blavatsky (978-1-63118-446-8)

Rosicrucians and Speculative Masonry in the Seventeenth Century (978-1-63118-489-5)

Qabbalistic Teachings and the Tree of Life by M P Hall (978-1-63118-482-6)

The Sepher Yetzirah and the Qabalah by M P Hall (978-1-63118-481-9)

The Devil in Love by Jacques Cazotte (978–1–63118–499–4)

Fortune-Telling with Dice by Astra Cielo (978-1-63118-466-6)

History, Analysis and Secret Tradition of the Tarot by Hall &c (978-1-63118-445-1)

Crystal Vision Through Crystal Gazing by Frater Achad (978-1-63118-455-0)

The Golden Verses of Pythagoras: Five Translations (978-1-63118-479-6)

Arcane Formulas or Mental Alchemy by W W Atkinson (978-1-63118-459-8)

The Machinery of the Mind by Dion Fortune (978-1-63118-451-2)

The A E Waite Reader: A Selection of Occult Essays (978-1-63118-515-1)

The Leadbeater Reader: A Selection of Occult Essays (978-1-63118-483-3)

Audio versions are also available on Audible, Amazon and Apple

Other Books in this Series and Related Titles

Philosophy of Self-Knowledge by Franz Hartmann (978-1-63118-613-4)

The Secrets of John Ernst Worrell Keely by Moore (978-1-63118-612-7)

Occult Symbolism of the Sun and Moon, the Goddess Isis and thee Solar Deities by Manly P Hall (978–1–63118–611–0)

Practical Theosophy by Annie Besant (978–1–63118–610–3)

The Human Body in Symbolism by Manly P Hall (978–1–63118–609–7)

Theosophical Basics by William Q Judge (978–1–63118–608–0)

The Hebrew Talisman by Richard Harte (978–1–63118–607–3)

Early Masonic Symbolism by Manly P Hall (978–1–63118–606–6)

Nature Spirits and Elementals by Louise Off (978-1-63118-605-9)

Swedenborg Bifrons by H P Blavatsky (978-1-63118-604-2)

Practical Use of Psychic Powers by C W Leadbeater (978-1-63118-603-5)

Using White & Black Magic by C W Leadbeater (978-1-63118-602-8)

Jesus, the Last Great Initiate by Edouard Schure (978-1-63118-599-1)

Mysterious Wonders of Antiquity by Manly P Hall (978-1-63118-598-4)

Ancient Mysteries and Secret Societies by Manly P Hall (978–1–63118–597–7)

The Zodiac and Its Signs by Manly P Hall (978–1–63118–596–0)

Life and Teachings of Hermes Trismegistus by Manly P Hall (978–1–63118–595–3)

The Secrets of Doctor Taverner by Dion Fortune (978–1–63118–594–6)

Vegetarianism, Theosophy & Occultism by Leadbeater &c (978–1–63118–593–9)

Applied Theosophy by Henry S Olcott (978–1–63118–592–2)

Higher Consciousness by C W Leadbeater (978–1–63118–591–5)

Audio versions are also available on Audible, Amazon and Apple

Table of Contents

Introduction...7

The Mysteries of Mithra

Preamble...9

Origins and Development...17

Diffusion in the Roman Empire...23

From the Texts...29

From the Monuments...37

INTRODUCTION

The word "esoteric" can be difficult to define. Esotericism in general can be seen less as a system of beliefs and more as a category, which encompasses numerous, different systems of beliefs. It's a bit of juxtaposition, since the word "esoteric" indicates something that few people know about, while the term itself broadly covers numerous philosophies, practices, areas of study and belief systems.

In a greater sense, Esotericism acts as a storehouse for secret knowledge, which is often considered ancient (by *tradition, if not by fact*), passed down from generation to generation, in private. At various times in history, simply possessing the knowledge of some of these subjects, was considered illegal and a jailable offence, if discovered. This usually included such general topics as Alchemy, Pharmacology, Qabalah, Hermeticism, Occultism, Ceremonial Magic, Astrology, Divination, Rosicrucianism and so on. Collectively, these areas of study were often referred to as the esoteric sciences.

Sometimes, the outer garment of a subject isn't esoteric, while what is hidden beneath it, is. As an example, Freemasonry isn't necessarily esoteric by nature (at *least not anymore*), but certain signs, passwords and handshakes given to the candidate during their initiation, are in fact, esoteric, in the sense that they are hidden from the general public.

Today, in the twenty-first century, such topics are readily available at bookstores across the country, and numerous main-steam publishers offer beginners guides and coffee-table volumes on many of these subjects, intended for mass appeal. Books like *"The Secret"* have turned previously arcane topics into household knowledge. All that being the case, however, it isn't to say that there still aren't buried secrets to uncover, ancient wisdom being ignored and forgotten mysteries to be explored. In fact, it is often that we are only able to further our own studies by standing on the shoulders of these disappearing giants.

Lamp of Trismegistus is doing its part to help preserve humanity's esoteric history by making some of these classics available to those students who are seeking to unearth the knowledge of these ancient colossi.

So, be sure to check other titles from our *Esoteric Classics* series, as well as our *Occult Fiction, Theosophical Classics, Foundations of Freemasonry Series, Supernatural Fiction, Paranormal Research Series, Studies in Buddhism* and our *Christian Apocrypha Series.* You can also download the audio versions of most of these titles from Amazon, Apple or Audible, for learning on the go.

THE MYSTERIES OF MITHRA

PREAMBLE

This brief outline of the comparatively meagre information we possess on what at one time was the most widely spread mystery-institution in the Roman empire, is introductory to the following small volume which will deal with the only Mithriac Ritual known to us.

In dealing with this exceedingly instructive Ritual I found that the limits of one booklet would not suffice for an adequate introduction; and without this, I fear, many readers will not be in a position to appreciate the Ritual at its just value.

For, in spite of the wealth of epigraphic and monumentary material now in our hands, the texts of the ancient writers which treat of the religion of Mithra, are, with rare exceptions, provokingly deficient in information on the doctrines and inner meanings of these famous Mysteries; and, therefore, a Ritual that unfolds to us the nature of the chief secret to which the lower grades of the mystery-rites conducted the brethren, is of the utmost value. It articulates, clothes with flesh, and puts life into what have been hitherto for the most part the dry bones of a skeleton.

And this, too, in spite of the splendid labours of the Belgian Hellenist Franz Cumont, who has done all that scholarship can do to make accessible to us every scrap of information on the subject that industry can discover.

The two sumptuous quarto volumes of Cumont's *Textes et Monuments figurés relatifs aux Mystères de Mithra* will long remain the most authoritative work on the subject; and the unstinted thanks of all who are interested in this fascinating study are due to Cumont for the admirable presentation of the labours which have occupied upwards of ten years of his life.

The second volume, which is embellished with no less than 493 figures and nine heliogravures, contains a reproduction of (i.) the literary texts--Oriental, Greek and Latin; (ii.) the inscriptions or epigraphic texts; and (iii.) the figured monuments and bas-reliefs; while the first volume, which contains fourteen additional figures and a map, is devoted partly to a critical introduction, in which this heterogeneous and puzzling mass of information is skilfully analyzed, and partly to the conclusions that may be drawn from the evidence.

Cumont has endeavoured rigorously to exclude any appearance of subjectivity from his judgments, and claims to have founded his conclusions on purely objective data. But when we remember that the secrets of the Mithriaca have been most strictly guarded by all the faithful, and that not even a single Church Father has been able to boast that he is in possession of their jealously guarded rites and doctrines, it will be seen that the elements of subjectivity and speculation must enter largely into the conclusions of even so rigid an objectivist as Cumont, at any rate as far as the rites and doctrines are concerned.

Again, it is the habit of most of those who follow the German school, in spite of the excellence of its methodology, to rest content when they have traced the elements of the main doctrines and features of a tradition to elements of a similar nature of an earlier date. If what are called "sources" and "prototypes" can be indicated, it is almost tacitly assumed that there is an end of the matter.

It is true that this is all the rigid adherents to pure objectivity can accomplish; but in the domain of religion it is with every day becoming clear that many doctrines which have been hitherto held to be direct physical derivatives from prior doctrines, have arisen independently owing to the natural evolution of the human soul and mind; that is to say, their source is subjective and not objective. The human soul has needs which it seeks to satisfy; and in all climes and times of similar stages of culture, similar means of satisfaction have been devised. And this simply because man is man.

The history of the evolution of the tradition of the Mithra-religion in Hither Asia, and of its continued development when it spread like wild-fire through the length and breadth of the Roman empire, in the first four centuries of our era, is an instructive study; but the main interest for many of us is the inner nature of the religion itself.

This, however, is a subject of extreme difficulty, as we have seen, owing to the jealously and secrecy with which its tenets were guarded. In spite of our more than 400 inscriptions, in spite of our upwards of 500 sculptures and bas-reliefs, we are unable to reconstruct the doctrines.

It is as though the living tradition and written records of Christianity had disappeared from the world for fifteen hundred years, and there remained to us only a few hundred monuments and the ruins of some three-score churches. What could we glean from these of the doctrines of the faith? How, from such meagre remains, could we reconstruct the story of the God, the saving doctrines, the rituals, the liturgies?

Nevertheless the fragments of information which can be gleaned from all this *débris* are of immense importance for the comparative history of religion, and throw light on many problems.

The Mithraism that spread over the Roman world in the first four centuries of our era, though it was the strongest, was not the only stream from the same source that reached the Western world.

Post-exilic Judaism was strongly tinged with Mazdaism, in the form of Pharisæism. Though it is strongly disputed by some, the Pharisees (Gk. Pharisaioi, Aram. Perishaya, Heb. Perushim) may have even owed their name to those whose doctrines they had partially absorbed; and Perashim may thus spell Persi in Hebrew transliteration, even as P~ rs§ does in India to-day.

But not only were the Pharisees, who gradually became the national party among the Jews, imbued with Mazdæan ideas, but many schools of a mystic and gnostic nature arose in Syria and Arabia who were more or less adherents of the Magian traditions, or influenced by Magian doctrines. Such schools formed one of the links between Jewish and Semitic Gnosticism on the one hand, and the Christianized Gnosis on the other.

It is to be remarked that Simon, whom the Church Fathers regarded as the earliest Gnostic heretic in Christendom, was surnamed the Magian, and that *The Great Announcement,* which was the principal document of the Simonian tradition, is filled with Magian doctrine.

Moreover the names of the Æons in a number of Christianized Gnostic systems, are those of ethical abstractions, precisely as are the names of the Amshaspands in the Avesta.

And not only are there distinct traces of this influence in some of the Christian Gnostic documents preserved to us, as for instance in the system underlying the Coptic Gnostic works contained in the Askew and Bruce Codices; but also we have many indications of a large literature derived from the doctrines of Zoroaster, and his Mazdayasnian successors, and directly attributed to him by the Greek writers.

This literature was in circulation among certain Christian Gnostic circles, and is also directly referred to by Porphyry, in his *Life of Plotinus,* when giving a list of the Gnostics against whom his master wrote one of the books of his famous *Enneads.*

Moreover the beautiful Syriac "Hymn of the Soul," which I have called elsewhere "The Hymn of the Robe of Glory," and which is almost certainly the work of the Christian Gnostic Bardaisan (Bardesanes), is thought by some to be based almost entirely on Magian doctrines. It may, therefore, contain valuable material for unveiling part of the inner secrets of Magianism, and, therefore, help us better to understand the innermost doctrines of the Mithriaca; and I hope to treat of it later in another small volume.

Though it is true that the religion of the conquering Achæmenidæ--the line of Cyrus, Darius, Xerxes, and the rest--did not have any effect on Hellas proper, it is highly probable that it did strongly affect the Hellenic cities of Asia Minor. Setting aside the statement that Pythagoras sojourned for years with the Magi at Babylon, and was initiated into their mysteries, it is for me almost indubitable that Heraclitus of Ephesus (*c.* 524-475 B.C.) was strongly imbued with Magian ideas; and not only was the influence of Heraclitus on subsequent Greek thought immense, but he was regarded by some Christian Gnostics and also by the Trismegistic tradition as one truly inspired by the Logos, and as therefore speaking true "logoi."

The conquest of Egypt, in the sixth century, by the Persian arms, moreover, cannot have failed to have made known to some extent the tenets of the Mazdæan faith in that land of lovers of religion, and to have awakened the curiosity of those learned in the mysteries of that land of wisdom in the allied teachings of the Magian priests.

Again, the conquest of the East by Alexander brought Greece into close contact with all the lands into which Magianism had directly spread itself, and this contact would aid in the diffusion of a knowledge of general Mazdæan tenets among the learned. Moreover, when Alexandria became the intellectual centre of the Grecian world, this interest in Magianism increased; and we learn that one of the librarians of the famous Brychion, Hermippus, the pupil of Callimachus, not only wrote a work in several books *About the Magi,* but, if we can believe Pliny, he catalogued the works of Zoroaster in the possession of the great Library, and found that they added up to the amazing total of 2,000,000 lines.

But Magianism did not reach Alexandria in its original form; it was already combined with many Chaldæan elements.

The "Books of the Chaldæans" also were well known at Alexandria; for Zosimus, the Pœmandrist, referring to the traditions of the Chaldæans, Parthians, Medes, and Hebrews, says that they were to be found "in the book-collections of the Ptolemies, which they stored away in every temple, and especially in the Serapeum."

The Serapeum was the second great building in which the world-famed Library was kept, when the rolls had grown too numerous for the Brychion.

Not only then were these Books in circulation in the original tongues in Syria, Palestine and Arabia, especially among the numerous mystic and gnostic communities, but also in Egypt. Zosimus, moreover, further informs us that they were translated into Greek and Egyptian.

It was on such translations, we must suppose, that the famous Greek poem known as *The Chaldæan Oracles* (and also as *the Oracles of Zoroaster*) was based. This was certainly in circulation in the second century, and may have existed earlier even in its present form.

When further we remember that, from the time of Porphyry onwards, the Later Platonic School esteemed these Oracles highly, and that at the same time Porphyry was intimately acquainted with the Mithraic Mysteries, and that the leading philosophers of the School were almost all Initiates of these Mysteries, we are not without hope of recovering the general drift of the main doctrines, on lines other than those Cumont has followed. But consideration of this side of the subject must be postponed until I come to deal with this poem itself in a subsequent volume.

All this shows that before the direct immigration of the Mithraic Mysteries (as known to us from the monuments) into the Roman empire, Magian doctrines had already strongly influenced Hellenistic religious thought.

As, however, we have already indicated, it is not to be supposed that the Magian doctrines of which we are speaking were of pure Iranian derivation. Magianism was already a blend. Irrespective of divisions and reforms within its own originally pure Aryan tradition, it had, from the days of Cyrus onwards, absorbed many elements from the astral lore and theurgic practices of the complex of Semitic religious traditions that formed the cults of Babylon. As so often happens in the world's history, the conquerors in war were subsequently conquered by peaceful means.

This stream of Magianism came direct from Babylon *viâ* Syria to Hellenistic Greece. The stream which we know later on as the Mysteries of Mithras, came by another way; it matured first of all especially in Armenia, Pontus, and Cappadocia (that is, Eastern Asia Minor), doubtless absorbing there some fresh elements from the indigenous cults, and eventually passed by way of the sea and military routes into the Roman empire.

Nevertheless the Mithriac tradition, in spite of its absorption and adoption of foreign elements, clung tenaciously to its ancestral myths and rites and doctrines, as constituting the real esotericism of its cultus; within them alone, it claimed, was to be discovered the *secretum secretorum* of its Mysteries.

The tradition of the Mithriaca, therefore, is of interest not only to students of the history of the influence of Oriental faiths on the culture and religion of the West, but should also be of value to the P~ rs§s, and to all students of the Zend and Pahlavi books, who generally hold that the Avestan tradition is indubitably in the main stream of direct Mazdæan descent; and that therefore the accounts of the Westeran classical writers are to be rejected when they do not agree with these documents.

On the other hand, it is a most remarkable fact that the Mithriac traditions possess features that more closely resemble the beliefs and practices of the Great Kings of the Achæmenid line, than do the Zend and still later Persian writings. Indeed no less an authority than Darmsteter has argued that Avestan Mazdaism was a later development, and as it were a systematized reform of Zoroastrian Magianism effected during the period of the Sassanid dynasty (226-628 A.D.). With this view Cumont agrees, and maintains that the Mithriac traditions preserve more of the earliest features of the original Iranian faith than do the Zend writings.

ORIGINS AND DEVELOPMENT

In the Magusæan tradition, that is the tradition of the Magians of Asia Minor, Mithra is all-important; in Avestan theology, the latest development of the great Zoroastrian reformation, Mithra holds but a subordinate place among the *yazatas,* or celestial deities, created by Ahura-Mazda.

It is, however, quite evident both from the oldest Vaidic hymns and the oldest traditions preserved in the Avestan documents, that in the beginning the God whom the Hymns call Mithra was one of the highest deities of a pantheon which was in prehistoric ages the common property of the forefathers of both the Iranian and Hindu Aryan races.

It is true that in the Zend books the ancient grandeur of the God is attested only by incidental allusions; but His attributes are such as to place Him on almost an equality with the Supreme.

In earliest days Mithra was God of Light, and was invoked together with Heaven (Zd. Ahura, Sk. Varuna).

In the Avesta, Mithra is Lord of the Heavenly Light, and therefore of the heavenly lights. He is the Light, and not the Sun; the Sun is His Chariot, or rather His Charioteer. He is "ever awake, ever on watch." He is neither sun nor moon nor stars; but with His "thousand ears and His ten thousand eyes" watches over the world. He hears all, sees all; no one can deceive Him. And so by a natural transition He is God of truth and loyalty; He is invoked in taking oaths, and guarantees all contracts and punishes all who violate their bond and plighted word.

And if He is Light, He is also Heat, and Life--the Vaidic K~ ma, the Orphic ErÇ s. He fecundates all Nature. Mithra is "the Lord of wide pastures"; 'tis He who makes them bring forth. "He giveth increase; He giveth abundance; He giveth herds; He giveth progeny and life." He poureth forth the waters, and causeth the plants to grow; He bestoweth on His worshippers health of body, wealth and well-dowered offspring.

In fact He is precisely what the worshippers of Osiris, and the followers of the Trismegistic tradition, and other Hellenistic cults, called AgathodaimÇ n or the Good Spirit, the Benefactor.

And not only does He bestow material benefits, but He also gives the good things of the soul--peace of heart, wisdom, and glory; He makes concord among the brethren who worship Him.

As God of Light He is the relentless foe of the Darkness and all its creatures--all suffering, sterility, vice and impurity. Against the forces of evil Mithra "sleeplessly on watch protects the creation of Mazda." He is the Leader of the hosts of Heaven against the hosts of the Abyss, and in all probability the prototype of Michael.

And in general it may be said that the picture which the Zend and Pahlavi books gives us of this ancient Aryan divinity is similar to the portrait with which the Vaidic hymns present us, though in the latter case with less clear detail.

But though the Zend G~ thas allow us to catch clear glimpses of the physiognomy of the Light-God, the Zoroastrian system, in continuing His cult, reduced the ancient grandiose conception of the God to somewhat meagre proportions, owing to the exigencies of the Avestan theology which placed Him among the *yazatas*.

Nevertheless every now and again the high rank of Mithra forces itself to the front in spite of all theological suppression, and we find Him several times joined with Ahura in one and the same invocation; the two forming a pair. Again it is said that though Ahura created Mithra as He created all things, nevertheless He made Him as great as Himself.

Mithra is a *yazata,* but at the same time He is the greatest of all *yazatas*. "Ahura-Mazda hath established Him to guard the whole world of life, and to watch over it." It is by means of this Mediator, the Evervictorious Warrior, that the Supreme Being destroys the demons (the *daevos* or *devs*) and causes the Spirit of Evil himself to tremble. The main outline of the Magian system which Plutarch hands on to us at the end of the first century, agrees with this, as also does the ancient tradition placed at the beginning of the later Pahlavi *Bundahish*.

This suggests that the fundamental religious conception of the subjects of the Achæmenid kings was simpler than the more complex and refined Zoroastrian theology. It presents us with a Supreme Deity throned above the stars in the Empyrean, reigning in eternal serenity and peace. Below Him stands an Active God, His Delegate, Mithra, Chief of the celestial armies in this perpetual struggle against the hosts of the Spirit of Darkness, who from the Abyss below the earth sends forth his *devas* to war on the "good creation" of Mazda.

From the inscriptions we know that the Great Kings (the Achæmenids) invoked Mithra alongside of Ahura-Mazda, and gave him special worship as their Protector. It was He who bestowed upon them the power of success, or the presence or glory, called HvarenÇ, which can be translated as "aureole." This Grace and Good Fortune of Mithra was a guarantee of perpetual victory. The epithet "most glorious," signifying the power of bestowing this HvarenÇ, was given to Ahura-Mazda and Mithra alone. Mithra in one of the Yashts is spoken of as He "who goeth through all the regions dispensing glory; . . . He goeth dispensing sovereignty and increasing victory."

The supremacy of Mithra is also shown by the enormous number of names of kings, princes and nobles containing the name of the God, and this not only in later days, but also in the earliest times.

The conquering kings of Persia established their religion wherever they carried their victorious arms. Especially at Babylon, which became the winter-residence of the Great Kings, was the Magian cult established in great splendour.

The Persian arms had laid low the temporal power that had previously reigned over the cities of the Chaldæi, and the priests of the conquerors, the Magi, were established in the highest place as the representatives of the religion of the Court. But the Iranian religion was not strong enough to resist the fascination of the ancient faith of the conquered that reached back, as it were, to the night of time, and preserved a science of the heavens that far surpassed the knowledge of the followers of Mazda. So strong was this influence that centuries later in Rome it was believed that the native land of Mithra lay on the banks of the Euphrates.

If we are unable to say that in Mesopotamia the religion of the Magi was entirely transformed, we can assert that it absorbed so many new elements that it assumed an entirely new form.

Of its spread eastwards we know little, though the astronomer Ptolemy assures us that Mithra was worshipped everywhere in all the lands from Assyria to India.

Babylon, however, was only the first stage in the propaganda of Mazdaism westwards, and also in its absorption of new elements. Under the Great Kings it spread rapidly into Armenia, Cappadocia, Pontus, Galatia, and Phrygia; and in these countries too we must believe it absorbed new elements from the ancient cults of these lands, and from the mystery-rites that handed on the inner instruction and preserved the secrets of the outer forms of worship.

In the great confusion that followed the downfall of the Persian empire, all political and religious barriers were broken down. Already to some extent Ionian philosophy had, in a few instances, felt the influence of general Magian ideas; but now in the train of the conquering arms of Greece, the influence of Greek civilization in its turn made itself felt on the Orient, and the Iranian princes and priests submitted to its charm.

The contact of all the religions of the "Orient" and of all the philosophies of Greece produced the most unexpected combinations. It was probably in the years following the Conquest of Alexander that the Magian priests departed from the reserve that they had hitherto maintained as far as Greece was concerned; for that reserve had been already broken down entirely with regard to the Chaldæan science, and doubtless to a large extent in the intercourse of the Magusæi with the initiatory cults of the more immediate countries north and west of Babylon.

Then it was that Mithraism blended with itself Grecian elements, and doubtless began to translate into Greek some of its rituals and liturgies, replacing the native names of its pantheon with what equivalents or approximations it could find in the names of the Olympian deities.

As Cumont writes, "it is certainly during the period of the moral and religious fermentation promoted by the Macedonian conquest, that Mithraicism received its more or less definitive form"--that is to say, the form in which it spread in the Roman empire.

This "synonomy," or translation of names, though perhaps necessary if the doctrines of Mithra were destined to spread widely in the West, was from a mystic or spiritual point of view unfortunate. For the vague personifications conceived by the Oriental imagination in no long time borrowed the precise forms with which the Greek art had clothed the Olympian gods.

Perhaps the Iranian deities had never previously been represented under a human form; if there had been images, they were probably similar to the "monstrous" or symbolic creations of the East, and of the same order as the awe-inspiring figure of the Æon which was still preserved in its original lineaments in the Mithræa.

And in the spread of the Mithriaca westwards, not only did art aid in softening what to those trained in Greek culture would appear to be the rudeness of these ancient Mysteries, but philosophy also was called in to help in the task; or rather the priests of the Invincible One, Nabarze, declared that in the best of philosophy were also to be found the secrets of their own sacred traditions.

The school whose tenets lent itself most easily to this purpose was that which later became the most popular of all among the cultured of the Roman world, the School of the Porch. When the cult of Mithra reached the upper classes of Roman society, after its first irruption among the soldiery and slaves, it was the adherents of the Stoic School who were most successful in finding in the dogmas and myths of the Magian tradition traces of an ancient wisdom consonant with their own ideas.

And in this connection it is of interest to repeat that the philosophy of Heraclitus had already strongly influenced the disciples of Zeno, the founder of the Wisdom of the Stoa, and that Heraclitus, who passed his life at Ephesus in the last quarter of the VIth and first quarter of the Vth century B.C., was almost indubitably indebted to Persian influence for his leading doctrines of the Ever-living Fire, of the transmutation of the Elements, of Struggle and Strife, and some other features of his remarkable system.

The analysis, therefore, of the compost of the Mithriac doctrines as propagandised in the Roman empire, presents us, as it were, with a series of stratifications. The deepest deposit belongs to the faith of ancient Iran; on this foundation of pure Mazdaism was deposited a thick layer of

Semitic doctrines from the ancient religions of Babylon; and on this again a shallower sediment of the cults of Asia Minor.

In this fertile soil, Cumont says, a luxuriant growth of Hellenic ideas sprang up and largely concealed from view its original nature. But if it is true that Mithraism in its contact with the West clothed its outermost form in Greek dress and with Greek art, it is equally true that it owed nothing of an essential nature to Hellenic notions. Its inner mystery-teachings were independent of Hellas; and any attempt to interpret these teachings from the standpoint of purely Hellenic ideas is doomed to failure.

Such was the composite faith--though hardly a Hellenized Parsism, as Cumont calls it--which flourished in the Alexandrine period in Armenia, Pontus and Cappadocia; and had Mithridates Eupator of Pontus realized his dreams of conquest, it would doubtless have become the religion of a vast Asiatic empire.

It was probably on the downfall of Mithradates that the *débris* of the Pontic armies and fleets spread the knowledge of the Iranian Mysteries among the sea-kings of Cilicia. Under the protection of Mithra these hardy adventurers pillaged without fear the most sacred sanctuaries of Greece and Italy; and so for the first time, it is said, the Latin world heard the name of the Conquering God (Per. Nabarze, the Courageous, Gk. Anik' tos, Lat. Invictus, the Unconquered) who was soon to receive the homage of the armies and navies of Rome, and finally of its emperors.

DIFFUSION IN THE ROMAN EMPIRE

It would be out of place in this short sketch to touch on anything but the main features of the diffusion of the Mithriaca in the Roman empire. The admirable account of Cumont, in the second chapter of his Conclusion, is practically exhaustive of the subject, and shows in detail, and with the aid of an excellent map, how the religion of the Victorious God spread into the most remote regions of the West, from the time that the Roman arms under Pompey, in the second quarter of the first century B.C., began seriously to undertake the conquest of the nearer East.

It was in Cilicia that Pompey's legionaries were first initiated into these Mysteries.

It is not surprising that the religion of Mithra should have found favour with the soldiery; for the cult of Victory was essentially a cult of warriors. Mithra was a warrior and a God of warriors; He was not only General of the celestial militia in the Good Fight, but also Protector of all brave deeds and chivalrous adventures.

It is a somewhat remarkable fact that the Magian influence in its earlier south-western diffusion, *viâ* Syria, Palestine and Egypt, seems to have been exclusively welcomed by strict ceremonialists like the Pharisees, or by mystic and ascetic communities of gnostic tendencies, or by circles of the learned at Alexandria; whereas in its direct spread westwards, it at first contacted a totally different stratum of society. It was welcomed at first almost exclusively by the common soldiery, and also by the slaves or those who had been freed by the state of servitude. The first propaganda of this second stream of Magianism thus followed the lines of the great military and trade routes.

The legions were being continually moved from station to station; corps raised in the East were, in accordance with the Imperial policy, despatched to the most distant provinces of the West; and the veterans on gaining their discharge either settled in the districts where they had last been stationed, or returned home, and so spread a knowledge of Mithra among their neighours.

Much of the trade in the great marts and factories was in the hands of Syrians and Levantines, whose chief commodity was the traffic of human flesh. The slaves brought from Asia Minor helped largely to spread the cult of Mithra among their fellows, and as many of them eventually held positions of responsibility in the management of the huge properties of the Roman nobles, they gradually succeeded in interesting their masters in their religion.

The above facts show very clearly that there were two distinct forms of Magianism that influenced the West; the one a doctrine better suited to priests and the learned, the other a teaching more adapted for warriors and the illiterate.

If we might so put it, one was of a Brahmana form, the other of a Kshattriya nature. The south-western stream seems to have been a form of Zoroastrian priestly Mazdaism; the direct western stream shows itself originally as a cult of kings and warriors, who exalted Mithra almost to equality with Ahura-Mazda.

The flood of Mithraism flowed with ever-increasing strength westward during the first and second centuries. It ascended the great rivers; and on the banks of the Danube, the Rhone, and the Rhine, it established its temples in great numbers. It penetrated to the North of Britain, to Spain, to the borders of the Sahara. Gradually it was established in all the great cities and trade centers, until with the third century we find it practically the dominant cult of the Empire, under the protection of the Imperial lords of Rome, whose claims to divine kingship were strongly supported by the tenets of a faith which attributed the power and victory of kings to the direct Favour and Glory of the God of Victory.

By this time, however, we have strong reason to suppose that the two streams of Magianism were, at any rate in some of the circles of the learned, flowing together. At any rate we see that in the case of Porphyry, at the end of the third century, this philosopher was not only learned in all that pertained to Mithra, but was also deeply versed in the Hellenized Mago-Chaldæan Oracles; and that from this time onwards the members of the Later Platonic school were mostly initiated into Mithraism and also great lovers of these Oracles.

Much has been written on the struggle between Later Platonism and Christianity for the possession of the Western world.

This Platonism was not a direct renascence of the older Platonism, but derived immediately from Alexandrian Hellenism. This Alexandrian Hellenism already consisted in a philosophizing of Oriental ideas--and among these ideas we must include a tincture of Magian tenets.

There is, therefore, little surprise that the most mystical school of Greek philosophy should have allied itself closely with the Mysteries of Mithra; and in so doing it supplemented its too aristocratic doctrines with ancillary tenets that had already found favour among the masses of the poor, the rude, and the unlettered.

But even so, neither Mithraism alone nor Neo-Platonism combined with it was destined to become the Faith of the West. It is true that in the years just prior to Constantine, the religion of Mithra seemed almost to have triumphed. But it was not to be; Christianity ascended the throne of the Cæsars, and Christianity became Cæsarized.

The daring effort of the Emperor Julian (A.D. 360-363) to re-establish the ancient order of things, or rather to save the ancient order by purifying it, and so winning the world to a loftier cult of the Gods, interpreted by philosophy and the mystery-teaching, collapsed; and with it passed the Gods from the Græco-Roman world.

Mithraism gradually faded out, or concealed itself in cognate Manichæism, which long survived as a harbour of refuge for the shipwrecked Gnostics and Mystics of the ancient world and early Middle Age.

Indeed the doctrine of Mani seems to have been in no small measure a third outpouring, so to speak, of Magianism. This outpouring blended itself intimately with the doctrines of the Christ-mystery, and even perhaps with Buddhism, and handed on a Gnosis that may ere long be better appreciated. For no less than 800 fragments of Manichæan MSS., in an ancient Persian dialect, have recently been discovered at Turfan in Chinese Turkestan, and are now at Berlin awaiting publication. As these are the only direct documents we possess of the religion of Mani--the rest of our information being derived from hostile sources--it is highly probable that we shall at last learn the true secret of its success, even as the Ritual we shall treat in our next volume, will enable us to see in some measure why Mithra exercised such sway over the hearts of His worshippers.

A certain form of Christianity conquered; that is to say, of all the various forms of faith in the West in those early years, Christianity in a certain form proved the most suited for the souls and minds of the coming nations. That form survived which was the fittest to survive for the instruction of the young nations which were gradually to develop into the ruling nations of the West. But that which withdrew did not die; it returned whence it came. It is there as it ever has been to reappear in other forms according to the birth, and growth and death of nations, and according to the coming and going of souls.

When souls are born who are not content with the forms of faith handed on by the ancestors of their bodies, their longing for what they consider new forms more suited to their needs, does but bring into manifestation once more the same Wisdom that instructed their spiritual forebears. We are to-day at an epoch when many such souls are in incarnation, and the interest in the doctrines of the Ancient Wisdom is accordingly increasing on all sides.

The religion of Mithra was one of the many forms of the Christ-mystery; and the mystery of the Christ is the mystery of man's perfectioning and final apotheosis. A comparative study of christology, in this its widest sense, and in all its manifold aspects, in the great religions that have disappeared or are still existing, is of the utmost value; and it is from this standpoint mainly that we are interested in the nature of the great secret of the Mithriaca.

The secret of regeneration, of being born anew, or spiritually, or from above--in brief, the divinizing of man, was the last word of the Mithra-rites; all else is introductory or ancillary.

This secret was the one secret of all the great mystery-rites and mystery-arts. It was the secret of the Gnosis in all its forms, contemplative or operative. We are, therefore, not surprised to learn that even as early as the end of the fourth century we find Zosimus, a disciple of the Trismegistic lore, and an alchemist, in a treatise "On Asbestos"--that is to say, presumably, on that pure body of man that can remain in the Fire without being consumed--writing as follows in mystic fashion:

"And if thou dry it in the sun thou shalt possess the mystery that no man can impart, in which no one of all the wisdom-lovers hath ventured to initiate in words; but only by the sanction of themselves [that is, the sanction of their own divinity] have they imparted its initiation. For this they have called in the scriptures the chief of all mysteries: The Stone that is no stone, the unknowable known unto all, the that which hath no honour yet is of greatest honour, the that which none can give but God alone. But I will sing its praise, the that which none can give but God alone, the one (material) thing in all our operations which is superior to all that is material. This is the remedy which doth contain all power--the Mithriac Mystery."

FROM THE TEXTS

In this short sketch it is only possible to dwell on one or two of the most striking passages from the classical writers.

Dion Chrysostom (*c.* 50-120 A.D.) was born at Prusa in Bithynia, travelled extensively in Asia Minor, and was very familiar with the Magian cult; in all probability he was himself an initiate of the Mithriaca. In one of his Orations, Dion hands on to us a very instructive mystery-myth which was chanted by the Magi in one of their sacred hymns.

They sang of the Supreme as the Perfect and Primal Charioteer of the Most Perfect Vehicle--more admirable and ancient far than the chariot of the sun which all can see. This Perfect Vehicle was the Cosmic Car drawn by the four Great Elements. It was the

All-perfect Sphere of the Æon, or Eternity; that is to say, of Boundless Time, who was also regarded by the Magi as Infinite Space. He is the Zervan Akarana, Eternity without Bounds, who in this tradition of Magianism transcended Ahura-Mazda Himself.

The Four Elements are the Steeds of the Great Chariot of all things. The course of the first Winged Horse is beyond the limits of heaven itself. This Steed transcends the rest in beauty, greatness and speed, and shines with purest brilliance. Its resplendent coat is dappled o'er with sparks of flame, the stars and planets and the moon. Such is the Steed of Fire.

The second Horse is Air. Its colour is black; the side turned towards its shining mate is bright with light, but that in shade is dark. In nature it is mild, and more obedient to the rein; it is less strong than Fire and slower in its course.

The third is Water, slower still than Air; while Earth, the fourth of this great Cosmic Team, turns on itself, champing its adamantine bit.

Round it its fellow Steeds circle as round a post. And this continues for long ages, during which the Cosmic Team work steadily together in peace and friendship.

But after many ages, at a certain time, the mighty Breath of the first Steed, as though in passion, pours from on high and makes the others hot, and most of all the last. And finally the fiery Breath sets the Earth Horse's mane ablaze. In the suffering of this cosmic passion the Earth causes such distress to its neighbour Steed and so disturbs its course, that exhausted by its struggles it inundates the Earth with floods of sweat.

This all happens at certain great periods of time when the Charioteer either reins in His Steeds or urges them on with the whip, as need may be to keep the world-course that His Will marks out.

But at the end of the world's age a still stronger mystery is wrought. A Divine Contest takes place among the Steeds; their natures are transformed, and their substances pass over to the mightiest of the Four. It is as though a sculptor had modelled four figures in wax, and melted them down again, and remade them into one form.

The One Element becomes omnipotent, and finally in its triumph is identified with the Charioteer Himself.

It is easy to see in this great myth, the periods of partial world-destruction by fire and water; and finally the re-absorption of all things in the Ever-living Element, now rebecome the One Element, the Single Body of all things.

To the Church Father Origen, writing some seventy-five years afterwards, we owe an important quotation from the *True Word* of the philosopher Celsus, who composed his criticism of Christianity about 175 A.D.

Origen, after telling us that Celsus is treating of the way of souls down and up through the planetary spheres, continues with a *verbatim* quotation as follows (vi., 22):

"These writings are symbolically set forth by the Wisdom of the Persians and the Initiation of Mithra which is practised among them. In the latter there is a certain symbolic representation of the two circuits in the heaven--both of the regular circuit and of that which is assigned to the irregular spheres--and of the passage of the soul through them.

"This symbolic representation is as follows: A ladder with seven gates, and at its top an eighth gate.

"The first of the gates is of lead, the second of tin, the third of copper, the fourth of iron, the fifth of alloy, the sixth of silver, and the seventh of gold.

"The first they assign as Saturn's, indicating by lead the slowness of the star; the second as that of Venus, setting in correspondence with her the brightness and softness of tin; the third of Jupiter, for it has a copper basis and is hard; the fourth as Mercury's, for both Mercury and iron are patient of work of every kind--the one transacts all business, the other is wrought with much labour; the fifth as that of Mars, for it is irregular from its mixture and variegated; the sixth as the Moon's, the silver one; and the seventh as the Sun's, the golden--in imitation of their colours."

Origen then tells us that Celsus gives further reasons for this arrangement, based on the symbolism of the names, and adds "musical reasons" as set forth in the "theology of the Persians."

This is the only description we have of the famous Mithriac Climax or Ladder, and it must be confessed that it leaves much to be desired. Whatever be the correct attribution of the metals to the "planets," and whatever may be the correct key to the alchemical or astrological secrets involved in it, it may be of interest to remark that this scheme was adopted as a means of theurgical yoga.

Mirrors of different metals were placed on the walls of an octagonal chamber, and in the centre was a couch, the legs of which were insulated. On this lay the seeker, and gazed into the mirror before him; in it he was supposed to see visions of invisible things, and develop in himself the senses of the soul.

My old friend and instructor had one of these chambers built shortly before her passing away, but it was never furnished, and so the experiment was not made. But recently a young friend of mine who had never heard of this, has had a dream-experience of a similar chamber, in which he seemed to have been once lying in Egypt. The couch on which he lay was a lion-couch.

The Church Fathers, however, seem to have had but the meagrest information on the Mithriaca.

Justin Martyr (*c.* 150 A.D.) says that the evil demons in the Mysteries of Mithra aped the Christian Eucharist; for there was an offering of bread and of a cup of water with certain explanatory sacred formulæ.

Tertullian in his exhortation *On the Crown,* written about 210 A.D., also accuses the Devil of aping some of the divine teachings in order to put the Christians to shame; and he instances certain of the Mithriac practices as follows (*c.* xv.):

"Blush, ye Fellow-soldiers of Christ, who need not be condemned by Him, but by any Soldier of Mithra.

"For when this Soldier is initiated in the Cave--in the Camp of Darkness as may well be said--and a crown is offered him at the sword's point--as though it were a mimicry of martyrdom--and then placed on his head, he is bidden to put up his hand and change it from his head to, it may be, his shoulder, declaring that Mithra is his Crown.

"And henceforth he never allows a crown [or wreath] to be put on him; and this he has as a mark whereby to prove himself, if on any occasion he should be tried concerning his mystery; immediately he is recognised as a Soldier of Mithra, if he cast down the crown, and declare that his Crown is his God."

Again in his treatise *On Prescription against Heretics* (c. xl.), Tertullian returns to the same convenient theory that the Devil by his wiles has perverted the truth, and "emulously mimics even the precise particulars of the divine sacraments by the mysteries of idols.

"He too baptizes some--of course his own believers and faithful; he promises the remission of sins by a bath. If I still remember rightly, Mithra there [that is in the Cave] signs his Soldiers on their foreheads, celebrates also the offering of bread, introduces an image of the resurrection, and purchases for himself a crown at the sword's point.

"What are we to say also of his appointing for his chief priest a single marriage only. He, too, has his virgins; he, too, has his celibates."

Augustine, at the end of the fourth century, in boasting that the Christian faith publishes and uncovers all the secret mysteries invented by the evil demons, instances the Mithriaca in the passage:

"But what kind of play is that which is played for them in the Cave with veiled eyes? For they have their eyes veiled lest they should shudder at the disgraceful dishonour to which they are put. Some like birds flap their wings imitating the cry of ravens; others again roar like lions; while others with hands bound with the entrails of fowls are made to leap over trenches filled with water, and then some one comes and severs the bond, and calls himself their liberator."

This apparently typified the effort of the soul, bound with the bonds of the passions, to overleap the watery regions, and gain the other shore, where the saviour severs the bonds with the sword of knowledge.

Lastly, Jerome, about the same date, in endeavouring to prove to a lady correspondent called Læta (Letter cvii.), that it is never too late to be converted, instances a certain patrician named Gracchus, "who had repudiated the Cave of Mithra and all the monstrous figures used in the initiations of the Raven, Griffin, Soldier, Lion, Persian, Sun-courser, and Father."

So much for the Fathers; as for the Philosophers, the one who tells us most about the Mysteries is Porphyry (*c.* 234-304 A.D.). His information is of importance not only owing to the reasons we have given above, but also because he was a careful student of a large literature on the subject which has since disappeared.

In his *Cave of the Nymphs,* and allegorical, philosophical and mystical interpretation of a famous passage in Homer, he tells us that the Ancients very properly symbolized the world by a cave, and then continues (c. vi.):

"Thus also the Persians, in their mystery-rites which give instruction on the path of souls in their descent to earth and the way out and up of their return, initiate the candidate (*myst' s*) in what they call the Cave.

"For, according to Eubulus, Zoroaster was the first who consecrated, in the mountains near Persia, a [certain] brilliantly coloured natural cave, with springs in it, in honour of Mithra, the Creator and Father of all things. This cave represented for him an image of the world which Mithra had made, and its regular stratification symbolized the cosmic elements and zones.

"After this Zoroaster, the practice was established among the rest [of the Magi] also of using grottoes or caves, either natural or artificially excavated, for the handing on of the mysteries."

In the Leontica or Lion-grade of the Mithriaca there was a honey-rite. To this Porphyry refers when he writes (c. xv.):

"The theologers have used 'honey' in many different symbolic ways owing to its being a same deduced from many powers, [and especially] because it has both a purifying and preservative virtue; for by honey many things are preserved from decay, and with honey long open wounds are purified. Moreover it is sweet to taste, and collected from 'flowers' by 'bees' who happen to be 'ox-born.' [These are evidently all mystery-terms.]

"When, therefore, they pour into the hands of those who are receiving the Leontic initiation, honey for washing instead of water, they bid them keep their hands pure from everything that causes pain or harm, or brings defilement; just as when the purifying medium is fire, they bring the candidate appropriate means of washing, declining water as inimical to fire.

"Moreover it is with honey too they purify their tongues from every sin.

"Further, when they bring honey to the Persian [that is, to the candidate who is being initiated in this grade, in the rites called Persica], as to the 'Keeper of the Fruits,' they symbolically signify the power of keeping [or preserving]."

The use of honey in the Leontica is corroborated by the engraved figure of a lion with a bee in its mouth. Nor is it easy in this connection, when we remember the bas-reliefs of the heroic deeds of Mithra, and the similar cycles of exploits of solar heroes, such as Nimrod, Gilgamesh and Hercules, to refrain from quoting the famous riddle put to Samson: "What is sweeter than honey? What is stronger than a lion?"

I also remember the mystic experience of a friend, who in a symbolic vision was chased by a great bee, and when in fear was told to let it suck his honey; after which a lion was sent to protect him, and he was told that he was being taught the veiling of the mystery. But to return to our text.

Porphyry then goes on to say that some think that honey further typifies the celestial nectar and ambrosia, and also the pleasure which draws souls down into generation. Then is the soul moistened and becomes watery; it is sucked down into the watery spheres within the great Cup or Crat' r of Generation; and so a crater or bowl is placed near Mithra to signify this.

"The Ancients moreover used to call the priestesses of Mother Earth (D' m' t' r) Bees, in that they were initiates of the Terrene Goddess, and the Maid (Kor') herself Bee-like. They also called the Moon the Bee, as Lady of Generation; and especially because [with the Magians] the Moon in exaltation is the Bull, and Bees are Ox-born--that is, souls coming into birth are Ox-born--and the 'God who steals the Bull' [Mithra] occultly signifies generation."

Further on Porphyry tells us that there are two entrances to the Cave; namely, the zodiacal Crab by which souls descend, and the Goat by which they ascend. By the northern gate the souls descend as men, by the southern they ascend to become gods. The northern regions and the southern are thus apportioned to souls descending into generation and then separating themselves from it (c. xx.).

"Hence they assigned to Mithra His proper seat upon the equinoctial circle." Thus astrologically interpreted, he may be said to bear the sword of the Ram, which is the martial sign, and to be borne upon the Bull, which is under the rule of Venus. And Mithra as well as the Bull is the Demiurge, or Creator, and Lord of generation.

One side of the Magian Mysteries, therefore, dealt with the descent of souls into generation, and the other with the ascent of souls and their freedom from the necessity of rebirth--that is, with their becoming gods. And this agrees with the nature of the Lesser and Greater Rites of all the great Mystery-institutions.

In his famous treatise *On Abstinence*, Porphyry further gives us a hint that the signs of the zodiac and the rest were but a veil to still more recondite secrets, in the following interesting passage (iv., 16):

"Among the Persians those who are wise concerning divinity and are servants of God, are called Magi; for this is the meaning of Magus in their native tongue. This race was considered so great and august among the Persians, that [King] Darius, son of Hystaspes, in addition to the rest of his titles, had engraved upon his tomb the fact that he had also been Master of the Magic [Mysteries].

"The Magi were divided into three castes, as Eubulus, who wrote the history of Mithra in many books, informs us. The first and most highly trained of them neither eat nor kill anything possessed of soul, but adhere to the ancient rule of abstinence from animals. The second [? the warriors] use flesh, but do not slay tame creatures. While the third [though they eat domesticated animals] do not use all of them as do the rest of the people.

"For the chief doctrine of all of them is that of metempsychosis. And this they also seem to make clear in the Mysteries of Mithra; for they are accustomed to indicate us [that is the grade or nature to which we belong] by means of animal forms, thus mystically symbolizing the nature which we have in common with the animals.

"Thus they call the initiates who take part in the actual rites Lions . . ., and those who serve [or the subordinates] Ravens. In the case of the Fathers moreover [the same symbolism is used], for they are called Eagles and Hawks.

"[These are the distinguishing marks of the three great grades]; in addition, he who receives the initiations in the Lion-grade is dressed in many animal-forms.

"And Pallas, in his books about Mithra, when giving the *rationale* of this, says that the general opinion would carry it right up into the zodiacal circle, whereas the true and correct reply declares that it has to do with the mystery of human souls which, they say, are clothed in bodies of every kind."

The above passages contain the most important scraps of information we can glean from the Greek and Latin texts. Owing to their fragmentary nature it is, of course, impossible to recover anything but a few scattered outlines of what must have been a very complex tradition.

There was in the East an elaborate public cult as well as an esoteric side of Mithraism; in the West there was nothing that can be called a public cult in any precise form, and no doubt, also, the mystery-rites were considerably modified to suit Greek and Roman ideas--at any rate in the exterior degrees of the general inner rites. Moreover, as they were introduced by the rough soldiery, these preliminary degrees retained or even exaggerated the rude features of the tradition; and it was only in the hands of the philosophers and the cultured that the inner rites contacted the deeper truths and intimate experiences which they were devised to veil and guard.

We will next turn to the evidence of the monuments.

FROM THE MONUMENTS

It is, of course, generally assumed that where there is any doubt between the evidence of the texts and the testimony of the monuments, the latter must decide the question. If, however, we should apply the same test to, say, Christianity, or to any other great religion in imagined similar circumstances, we see at once that the monuments would by no means be the more important witnesses; indeed they would be frequently very misleading. What, for instance, could we make out of the Stations of the Cross, if we possessed no single word of the Gospel story? What, from the naïve mediæval figured representations of the Creator, could we divine concerning the true attributes of the Supreme?

Of all the sculptured figures discovered in the ruins of the Mithræa, the most extraordinary, and even awe-inspiring, is the symbolic statue of the mysterious Æon, transcending gods and men. He is the Everlasting One, the Lord of Light and Life--the Autozoon, He that gives life to Himself, and is the Source and Ender of all lives. He is Zervan Akarana, Boundless Time, and also Infinite Space, the Ingenerable and Ineffable, the Pantheos.

The rest of the Mithriac sculptures are disguised by the genius of Greek art, which in beautifying the originals and humanizing the symbolic creations of Oriental imagination deprived them of their mysterious nature. The Æon alone remained intractable to the ingenuity of Hellenic iconography.

This mysterious figure is that of a "monster" as it is called; or rather it typifies the source or prototype of all ensouled forms including that of man.

The body is that of a man, and is frequently covered with the signs of the zodiac.

The feet are sometimes human, sometimes animal, sometimes they end in the coils of a serpent.

In all cases there is a huge serpent coiled round the body of the Æon, generally in seven coils; and the head of the serpent lies on, or curves over, the head of the statue, and in one case bends round into the Æon's mouth.

The head of the figure is that of a lion thickly maned.

From the shoulders spring two wings upwards, and below these two wings hang down. These are sometimes decorated with symbols of the four seasons.

On the breast is the sacred bolt of power, and in either hand a key, while the right holds a sceptre or rod as well.

This startling image generally stood on the celestial sphere; occasionally other symbols were added to the pedestal--such as the serpent-rod of Hermes, the cock of Asclepius, the tongs and hammer of the Fire-god, Hephæstus, and the pine cone. All these symbols are connected with the creative power.

The Æon therefore typified the power of all things and of all gods. The Æon was Lord of the whole Celestial Sphere, and of the Four Great Elements. The serpent symbolized earth; the head of it entering the mouth is paralleled by a number of monuments on which the serpent drinks from a crater or water-vessel; the wings symbolize air; and the lion-head with its shaggy mane typifies fire and light.

The keys are the keys of life and death, of light and darkness, of all the opposites. The bolt and sceptre are the emblems of supreme power.

But the Æon was not only a symbol of the cosmogonical power of the creator. The promise that was gradually revealed to the initiate was that he might not only see the Æon in all His glorious actuality, but finally become the Æon. There was not only instruction as to the way down, but also precise doctrine as to the way up.

Man was destined to become the Æon by making his own body cosmic as was the Body of the Æon. There was a Perfect Body in man hidden in the imperfection of his partial frame. The serpentine power and all the other powers were to come to birth in him when the time appointed by the Æon should be fulfilled.

Of the rest of the monuments the chief was the group of the Bull-slaying Mithra. In every Cave this formed the chief object, and it was placed in the apse of the subterranean temple like a modern reredos.

Within a sculptured frame representing a natural cave, the ever-young God, with averted face, as though in sorrow, plunges his short sword, or broad sacrificial knife, into the heart of the Bull, grasping its nostrils with the left hand, and with his left knee upon the back of the kneeling beast.

Mithra is clad in trowsers and a single robe girdled round the centre, and with a mantle flying in the wind, as though it were the wings of an eagle settling on its prey. This mantle or cloak is generally covered with constellations. On his head is a Phrygian cap.

The blood that flows from the wound of the Bull is sometimes represented by bearded ears of corn, and frequently the tuft of hair at the end of the Bull's tail is also composed of similar wheat-ears.

A dog, the symbol of instinct and watchfulness, laps the blood; while below the smitten beast is a serpent and a crat' r, or water-vessel, and a scorpion seizes the generative parts of the Bull.

On either side are two smaller figures, almost duplicates of Mithra; one holds a torch upwards, the other a torch reversed. These dadophors or torchbearers represent the powers of life and death, of waking and waning, of spring and autumn, of ascent and descent. They are also symbols of the two great powers represented, in the Alchemical and Rosicrucian tradition, by the right hand raised with finger pointing upwards, and the left down with finger pointing downwards--accompanied by the mystic utterances Coagula and Solve; Collect and Disperse, Fix and Volatilize.

This famous artistic group was based on an Attic original by an artist of Pergamum in the second century B.C. The original was a bas-relief which ornamented the balustrade of the temple of Athena-Nik'on the Acropolis--the well-known figure of Victory sacrificing a bull.

But the group of the Tauroctonous Mithra was significant of greater things.

According to the Avestan tradition the first living creature created by Ahura-Mazda was a Bull. The Spirit of Opposition, Ahriman, oppressed it with every ill and finally compassed its death; but, marvellous to tell, from its body sprang up the whole vegetable kingdom.

In the Mithriac tradition, in which we find scarcely any reference to Ahriman, the mystery is otherwise explained. It is the Vice-regent of the Supreme who accomplished the primal sacrifice. This is depicted admirably by the artists who delineated the look of regret and remorse on the face of the God, sacrificing His own most prolific creation that greater benefits might be showered upon the barren earth.

The wheat-ears typify vegetation on the one hand and also the spermatic power of the creative life on the other. Moreover the *Bundahish* tells us precisely that when the Primal Bull was slain, all the different species of plants sprang from the different parts of its body, and especially from its spinal marrow.

But this was not all. If there were mysteries of generation, cosmic and human, there were also mysteries of regeneration. There was a christology and soteriology as well as a cosmology.

We know from our texts that the ancient Persians believed in a resurrection of the dead, and the Mazdæan books prophesy that at the last day the Saviour Saoshyañt will slay a Bull, and from its fat mingled with the juice of the white Haoma (the Indian Soma, replaced in the West by Wine) will prepare a Draught of Immortality for all men.

But the highest initiates of Mithra knew that the last day was for every man when the Æon gave command; and that Mithra as Creator was ever slaying the Cosmic Bull, and Mithra the Saviour was ever slaying the Bull of Generation in the presence of His true worshippers. The Draught of Immortality was ever ready for him who had made himself ready.

But the Tauroctonous group though the central one, was not the only scene depicted on the Mithriac reredos.

Besides various symbolical representations connected with the sun, moon and planets, etc., there are two series of tableaux which specially invite our attention. It is, of course, somewhat rash, in the absence of all confirmatory texts, to hazard a suggestion of anything but the main purport of these two series of scenes.

The first consists of six scenes; the second of ten. The first is apparently a history of cosmogenesis; the second is clearly a pictorial memorial of the exploits of Mithra.

I. *THE COSMOLOGIC TABLEAUX*

1. The first tableau consists of a full face, surrounded by a thick encircling which appears to be divided into eight parts. This is evidently the primordial deity; in its solitariness doubtless the Æon, but taken in connection with the next scene it is Heaven.

2. For the second tableau represents a woman, with the upper part of her body naked, reclining on the earth; her left hand touches a basket of fruits, her right is raised above her head. Near her is the figure of a man, visible only as far as his waist, who supports a great sphere on his head. This Atlas is clearly Heaven and the recumbent figure Earth--the primordial pair.

3. Then follows a male figure half recumbent on the rocks; a similar figure sometimes appears with water flowing at his feet. This is clearly Ocean; and the Avestan tradition has preserved the ancient saying: "All was created from water." Did Thales, then, derive his leading dogma from Iranian mythology?

4. Next comes a group of three female figures in long robes. They are the triple Fortune or Fate, who was regarded in Persia as the daughter of Heaven and Earth. All the above related to the night of time, during the reign of Zervan.

5. For the next scene depicts Zervan (Kronos) handing over to Mazda (Zeus) the sovereignty of the world.

6. Finally, we have a scene which depicts Ahura brandishing his thunderbolt and hurling down from heaven the rebellious giants.

II. *THE HEROIC TABLEAUX*

1. The first scene represents the birth of the God from a rock. This stone was called the Generative Rock. Frequently this rock is surrounded by a serpent raising its head towards the child, whose body is naked, and only half out of the stone. On his ringlets he wears a Phrygian cap, and carries in the right hand a knife and in the left a torch.

The cosmogonic interpretation connects this birth from the rock with the birth of light from the firmament which was regarded as solid in Iranian tradition, while the solar interpretation would refer it to the rising of the sun from behind the mountains. But let us come to something nearer home. Our tableau seems to represent a greater mystery--the birth of what may be called the first spark or again the first outpouring of life on earth.

If we may elaborate somewhat the mystery of that which sleeps in the mineral, wakes in the animal, and is perfected in man, it might be said that the first light-spark, or life-stream, according as we regard it in its masculine or feminine potency, is passive or sleeps in the mineral and is active or wakes in the vegetable.

The second spark, or the intensification or power of the first, sleeps in the animal and wakes in man; while the third is the mystery of what Basilides would call the third "sonship," which is that of Christhood.

2. It is, therefore, of interest to remark that next to the tableau of Mithra Petrogen's comes a scene in which there is a great tree with leafy branches extending to the top of the picture. Before it is standing a young man, quite naked, except for his Phrygian cap. He is cutting from the tree a branch covered with leaves and fruit. The spark becomes active in the vegetable kingdom on earth; it plants there a branch from the tree of life.

Often in this same scene is seen a figure clothed in an oriental tunic half issuing from the leafage of the tree, while another figure blows or breathes straight in his face. This is evidently a different incident in the cycle of experience, and the two scenes were sometimes depicted apart. It seems clearly to represent the passage from the vegetable to the animal kingdom, and the inbreathing of the second spark, the breath of lives, the animal soul. The naked first spark is half clothed by the second.

3. The next tableau represents a young man clad in an Asiatic costume and wearing a Phrygian cap, the usual full clothing of Mithra. He holds in his hand a bow and shoots an arrow at a lofty rock. Where the arrow hits the rock there cascades forth a spring of water. A kneeling figure catches the stream in the palms of his hands and drinks of the water greedily.

This seems to represent the coming to birth of the generative power, and animal nature in man. It may even hide an ancient mystery tradition that man was born before the animals on earth, and through his greedy delight in the passion nature of the watery planes, he produced the animal world as known on earth. However this may be, the symbolism seems to suggest that the water is the stream of genesis and that man is absorbed in its delights. There is as yet no war in his members; he is the natural primitive animal man.

4. With the next tableau the order changes, and the Bull is brought upon the scene.

First of all we have two representations which are closely connected, and are always found together when they occur on the same monument, though one of them sometimes is found alone. A kind of wherry which appears to float upon the waters, bears on it, either standing or lying down, the mythic Bull.

Alongside of this scene, is another consisting of a little gabled house from which the Bull is ready to leap. One of the monuments gives us the reason of this leaping forth. Two persons, of whom one is indubitably Mithra, seem to be applying torches to the roof and door of this byre.

This seems to suggest the descent and the rousing into activity of the animal generative power under the fervent heat of the divine impulse.

5. We next come to a series of scenes variously depicted, but all connected with the contest of Mithra with the Bull.

First the sacred animal is seen browsing quietly in a meadow, or raising its head as though to listen.

Then Mithra comes on the scene. Sometimes he is seen carrying the Bull on his shoulders, like the Good Shepherd with the lamb, or Hermes Criophorus with the kid; he turns his head as though he feared pursuit.

Sometimes he walks alongside of the beast, holding its horns; again he mounts astride upon it and rides it quietly, guiding it with one hand by means of its nostrils.

In another scene the Bull starts off in a wild gallop; Mithra with his arms round its neck lies flat along its back as though all but swept off by its rush; sometimes he has fallen and only just saves himself by clinging desperately to its horns.

At last, however, the fierce animal is conquered; the God takes it by its two hind feet over his shoulders, and drags it off, with its front hoofs trailing on the ground. He thus carries it to the cave where he is finally to slay it.

Whatever other interpretations there may be of this most famous exploit of the God, it seems very clear that it chiefly signified the conquest of the irrational nature by the reason, and the final reversal of the latter,-- the beginning of the ascent, the true "repentance," or "conversion."

But to me it seems to indicate as well certain processes of mystic physiology or psycho-physiology. What I have called a spark (following a certain gnostic nomenclature) is really a power or substance hidden in every atom of the body, and is only graphically spoken of as one spark or atom.

These scenes in which Mithra grasps the horns of the Bull, seem to signify the marriage of what might be called an atom of the mental nature with an atom of the passional nature. There is struggle, there is conquest, and finally there is death prior to resurrection.

The passional nature is converted, led back by the initiate into the cave in the depth of his own substance, there to be slain--"the lamb slain from the foundation of the world"--and from its blood will spring up the plants and trees of life, and it will give corn with which to feed the hungry with the bread of life.

6. The next group depicts Mithra holding in his right hand above his head the shoulder of a calf; kneeling before him is a young man naked, or in a simple chlamys, raising his hands in sign of supplication. With this must be taken a similar scene in which Mithra apparently lays aside the object in his right hand, and with his left places on the suppliant's head a radiant crown; while again in another scene he lays his left hand on the head of the sword at his waist, and the crown lies on the ground between them.

The shoulder of the calf is, in celestial imagery, the symbol of the seven stars of the constellation of the Bear which were supposed to turn the great sphere. These are the Lords of the Pole, and Mithra is their Lord. The seven jewels, representing the seven simple senses of the celestial or spiritual body, are now ordered in the initiate's heaven and he is crowned with the Sun.

7. The next scene represents a compact or bond of brotherhood between Mithra and the Sun. Perhaps this represents the grade of the Heliodromos, or Sun-courser, as I have translated it above in the passage from Jerome; of the man whose course is now as the course of the stars in high heaven.

8. Whether or not this scene is here in the right order, it is impossible to say. It represents what is apparently Mithra's Hunting. The God is

mounted on a horse in full gallop; his cloak flies in the wind behind him and he shoots his arrows, while an attendant follows with a quiver of darts.

This seems to suggest the activity of the perfect man, mounted on the white steed of purified passion, and directing his powers against the forces of evil; the attendant is perhaps the Sun, who supplies him with his arrows.

9. The next tableau depicts a feast. Mithra and the Sun are seated on a cushioned couch with a table before them on which are loaves, quartered by a cross, and they hold goblets in their hands. Surrounding them, and serving them apparently, are symbolic representations of the initiates of various degrees--such as the Raven, Persian, Soldier and Lion--and below the latter are some of the sacred animals, notably the Bull; indeed, from one of the greater monuments it seems as though the Bull's back formed the table of this final Banquet or Agapʻ.

This feast perhaps pertained to the Master-grade alone; it could only be partaken by the Fathers.

10. The last scene depicts the Departure of Mithra, in the Chariot of the Sun, towards the Region of the West, represented by the figure of Ocean. It is the *consummatum est;* He goes unto His own.

One is well aware that these mythic scenes can be interpreted in many other ways, according to the number of times there may be power to turn the key. One is also well aware how hazardous is the present undertaking in the absence of all documents. But as there is confidence that all the great Mystery-traditions set forth chiefly the Mystery of Man, I have ventured to suggest the above interpretation from what I have gleaned of other similar traditions and a comparative study of the Gnosis.

From this brief sketch I have been compelled to omit a thousand points of interest and a thousand puzzles of scholarship. But as there has been no intention of writing an elaborate treatise, but only the object of getting as much of interest as one could into these few pages, as introductory to the more definite subject of the Ritual which Dieterich has rescued from the chaos of the famous Greek Magic Papyrus of Paris, I must now break off, and reserve what else there may be to say for the next small volume.

www.ingramcontent.com/pod-product-compliance
Lightning Source LLC
LaVergne TN
LVHW041502070426
835507LV00009B/753